FRENCH
COOKBOOK

60 Recipes for Traditional Food from France

Adele Tyler

© **Copyright 2022 by Adele Tyler - All rights reserved.**

This document is geared towards providing exact and reliable information in regard to the topic and issue covered. The publication is sold with the idea that the publisher is not required to render accounting, officially permitted, or otherwise, qualified services. If advice is necessary, legal or professional, a practiced individual in the profession should be ordered.

From a Declaration of Principles which was accepted and approved equally by a Committee of the American Bar Association and a Committee of Publishers and Associations.

In no way is it legal to reproduce, duplicate, or transmit any part of this document in either electronic means or in printed format. Recording of this publication is strictly prohibited and any storage of this document is not allowed unless with written permission from the publisher. All rights reserved.

The information provided herein is stated to be truthful and consistent, in that any liability, in terms of inattention or otherwise, by any usage or abuse of any policies, processes, or directions contained within is the solitary and utter responsibility of the recipient reader. Under no circumstances will any legal responsibility or blame be held against the publisher for any reparation, damages, or monetary loss due to the information herein, either directly or indirectly.

Respective authors own all copyrights not held by the publisher.

The information herein is offered for informational purposes solely and is universal as so. The presentation of the information is without contract or any type of guarantee assurance.

The trademarks that are used are without any consent, and the publication of the trademark is without permission or backing by the trademark owner.

All trademarks and brands within this book are for clarifying purposes only and are owned by the owners themselves, not affiliated with this document.

CONTENTS

INTRODUCTION 8

CHAPTER 1: TRADITIONAL PARIS AND ÎLE-DE-FRANCE RECIPES 13

BAKED CAMEMBERT OR BRIE WITH ENDIVES 14

BAKED APPLE BRIE 15

HOMEMADE ILE FLOTTANTE 16

BOUCHEESA A LA REINE 18

BUCHE DE NOEL 19

PARIS BREST 20

CROQUE MONSIEUR 22

BRAISED DUCK WITH CHERRIES 24

APPLE TART (BOUQUET DE ROSES) 25

VEAL STEW 26

CHAPTER 2: TRADITIONAL CHAMPAGNE, LORRAINE, AND ALSACE RECIPES 28

ALSATIAN CHEESE TART 30

QUICHE LORRAINE 32

BUTTERMILK-SPINAC SPAETZLE 34

CHICKEN IN RIESLING WITH CABBAGE AND PRUNES 35

BOUDIN BLANC DE RETHEL 36

KIR ROYALE 37

CHAPTER 3: TRADITIONAL NORMANDY, AND BRITTANY RECIPES 39

NORMANDY FRENCH ONION SOUP 40

DUCK NORMANDY 42

NORMANDY PORK WITH PORK & CIDER 44

BRITTANY CAKE 45

BRITTANY COOKIES 46

POULET A LA BRETONNE 48

CHAPTER 4: TRADITIONAL LOIRE VALLEY AND CENTRAL FRANCE RECIPES 50

CHEESECAKE RECIPE FROM LORRIE VALLEY 51

LORRIE VALLEY PORK RILLETTES 52

CHARD ROASTED SALMON WITH FENNEL SALAD 54

BUCKWHEAT CREPES WITH CREAMY LEEKS AND BAKED EGGS 55

LUDO LEFEBVRE'S OMELET 56

THE LOFFTIEST SOUFFLE 58

CHAPTER 5: TRADITIONAL BURGUNDY AND FRANCHE-COMTÉ RECIPES 60

GASTON GERARD CH8CKEN 61

POULET A LA COMTOISE 62

BREADED COMTE BITES WITH ESPELLETE PEPPER CREAM 64

DIJON GINGERBREAD 65

DIJON PEAR SALAD 66

DIJON NONNETTES 68

CHAPTER 6: TRADITIONAL BORDEAUX, PÉRIGORD, GASCONY, AND BASQUE COUNTRY RECIPES 70

BASQUE POTATO AND PEPPER TORTILLA WITH HAM AND CHEESE 71

BASQUE CHERRY PIE 72

BAYONNE HAM OMELET 74

POULET AU POT WITH GROSS SEL SAUCE 75

FRENCH TOMATO TART 76

PRUNE FLAN 78

PASCAL AUSSIGNAC LE FAMEUX CASSOULET 79

BAKED WHOLE TRUFFLES IN SALT 80

BALLOTINE DE POULET 81

CAP FERRET OYSTERS 82

CHAPTER 7: TRADITIONAL PROVENCE-ALPES-CÔTE D'AZUR RECIPES 85

FRENCH BOUILLABAISE 86

FRENCH PASTIS 88

FRENCH DAUBE 89

FRENCH TAPENADE 90

FRENCH NOUGAT 92

OMELETTE AUX TRUFFLES 93

FRENCH RATATOUILLE 94

FRENCH AIOLI 96

TARTE TROPEZIENNE 97

FROMAGE DE CHEVRE 98

CHAPTER 8: TRADITIONAL CORSICA RECIPES 101

BROCCIU CHEESE AND MINT OMELET 102

CORSICAN MINESTRA 103

CORSICAN LASAGNE 104

ROUGETA A LA BONIFACIENNE 106

CIVET DE SANGLIER 107

GATEAU A LA FARINE DE CHATAIGNE 108

CONCLUSION 112

Introduction

As perhaps the best food on the planet, French cooking is remembered to be one of the healthiest eating regimens. From tasty ocean bottom to meat dishes, excellent cheddar to scrumptious cakes, and the best wines to enjoy - French food is the best. Would you like to dive more deeply into French food's historical aspect and ingredients? Keep perusing to dive further into it!

In all honesty, there is a novel method for eating bread in France. No snacking on the bread before your feast shows up. Bread is a staple of French cooking and one of a handful of the food sources that should be eaten with your hands. Utilize the bread to plunge into any sauces that are given and to clean your plate. This act shows that you have an authentic appreciation for the dinner.

As the third biggest country in Europe after Ukraine and Russia, France is completely encircled by a wealth of mountains. France's ideal environment and rich soil are made for cultivating, from vegetables to grapes for wine. All things considered, France is an independent country with food and liquor assuming significant parts in French society for ages.

Back in the days of yore, how an individual would eat would mirror their French legacy, economic wellbeing, and physical wellbeing. For instance, King Louis XIV (1661-1715) would hold twelve-hour feasts with more than ten different top-notch dishes served. Such intricate banquets were too costly and required an excessive amount of time for the folks to prepare, yet such feasts would be regularly appreciated among privileged residents.

French food is famous for wine and cheddar, yet it is about considerably more wonderful fixings. Olive oil is utilized in many French dishes, from different vinaigrette to dressing for salad recipes or main dishes. Dijon mustard is a smooth, gentle kind of mustard with a sprinkle of vinegar. Dijon mustard is utilized for different purposes, beginning from thickening vinaigrette or just to thickening a marinade. The truffle flavor is utilized broadly in many French plans. Truffle oil, for example, is a significant part of French recipes. The creme fraiche is generally utilized for different recipes, be it soups, bread shop merchandise, madeleines, macaroons, and many dishes. Herbes de Provence incorporates oregano, rosemary, thyme, and tarragon are other normally utilized spices. These spices are utilized to prepare flavorful vegetable dishes.

This book contains 60 easy-to-make recipes belonging to different cities of France. The recipes are categorized as belonging to Paris, Île-de-France, Champagne, Lorraine, Alsace, Normandy, Brittany, Loire Valley, Central France, Burgundy, Franche-Comté, Bordeaux, Périgord, Gascony, Basque country, Provence-Alpes-Côte d'Azur, and Corsica recipes. You will definitely become a French cooking expert with this cookbook. Keep reading!

Chapter 1: Traditional Paris and Île-de-France Recipes

Food preparation and French cooking are inextricably linked. French cuisine boasts a long and illustrious culinary history including natural home cooking, elaborate court-feasting showpieces, and cutting-edge Parisian haute cuisine. The craft of flavorful food is developed close by vegetables, organic products, and sauces in Île-de-France and Paris. These two cities were the lords of France's jungle, as they both had a varied scene of backwoods and fields. Among this scenic natural beauty, little wonders in the form of delicious food sprouted up in both the cities. Follow the recipes below to make delicious food at home:

BAKED CAMEMBERT OR BRIE WITH ENDIVES

INGREDIENTS

- Four small endives
- One brie cheese or camembert cheese

COOK TIME: *20 mins*
SERVING: *4*

INSTRUCTIONS

1. Preheat the broiler at 150 degrees.
2. Begin by discarding the paper that the brie is placed in and setting the brie back in the wooden box with just the base revealed.
3. Bake the brie on a baking plate or in a tin for around twenty minutes.
4. Meanwhile, wash the endive and organize them with the cheddar confine top the middle and the leaves all over.
5. When the cheese is liquefied, place it on the plate.
6. Serve hot!

BAKED APPLE BRIE

INGREDIENTS

- A quarter cup of dried cranberries
- One tablespoon of butter
- One tablespoon of brown sugar
- A quarter teaspoon of ground cinnamon
- A quarter cup of chopped pecans
- One brie cheese
- One cup of apple slices
- A pinch of nutmeg
- Crackers for serving

COOK TIME: 20 *mins*
SERVING: 10

INSTRUCTIONS

1. Preheat the broiler to 150 degrees Celsius.
2. Dissolve the margarine in a pan over medium heat.
3. Cook and mix the walnuts, apple, cinnamon, cranberries, brown sugar, and nutmeg for five minutes, or until the apple slices are delicate.
4. Place the Brie in a pie plate.
5. A big part of the apple blend should be put on top.
6. Wrap up with the remainder of the apple blend.
7. Heat uncovered for ten minutes, or until the cheddar starts to liquefy.
8. Serve hot with crackers.

Tip: Make sure you do not take green apples for this recipe.

HOMEMADE ILE FLOTTANTE

INGREDIENTS

- **For the meringue:**
- One cup of icing sugar
- Two egg whites
- One cup of sugar
- Pralines for serving
- Salt to taste
- **For the custard:**
- One vanilla pod
- Two cups of milk
- Five egg yolk
- Half cup of sugar

COOK TIME: 20 *mins*
SERVING: 4

INSTRUCTIONS

1. Take a large pan.
2. Add the milk and sugar into the pan.
3. Mix the ingredients well and add the egg yolks and vanilla pod into the pan.
4. Mix all the ingredients well to form a thick custard.
5. Pour the custard into a bowl when done.
6. Take a large bowl.
7. Add the egg whites and salt into the bowl.
8. Beat the egg whites well and then add the icing sugar into the bowl.
9. Beat the mixture well until the eggs turn stiff.
10. Add the meringue on top of the custard with the help of a pipping bag.
11. Take a pan.
12. Add the sugar into the pan.
13. Melt the sugar.
14. Cook the sugar well and then use a spoon to add the melted sugar on the meringue.
15. Your dish is ready to be served.

BOUCHEESA A LA REINE

INGREDIENTS

- Two tablespoons of olive oil
- Two teaspoons of chopped garlic
- One cup of sliced button mushroom
- Four large pastry sheets
- Two cups of saucy supreme
- Half cup of chicken stock
- Salt to taste
- Black pepper to taste
- One teaspoon of de beurre
- Two tablespoons of chopped onions
- One cup of chopped chicken fillet
- One teaspoon of espelette pepper

COOK TIME: 30 mins
SERVING: 4

INSTRUCTIONS

1. Take a pan.
2. Add the olive oil, and onions into the pan.
3. Cook the onions until they turn soft.
4. Add the minced garlic, chicken pieces and button mushroom slices into the pan.
5. Cook well.
6. Add the espelette pepper, de beurre, salt and black pepper into the pan.
7. Cook the ingredients well and add the chicken stock into the pan.
8. Cook the chicken pieces for ten minutes.
9. Dish out when done.
10. Cut the pastry sheets in half.
11. Stuff the formed mixture on the pastry sheets.
12. Roll the pasty sheets and close the open ends with a fork.
13. Place the pastries on a greased baking dish.
14. Drizzle saucy supreme on top.
15. Bake the pastries for thirty minutes.
16. Dish out when the pastries turn golden brown in color.
17. Your dish is ready to be served.

BUCHE DE NOEL

INGREDIENTS

- Half cup of icing sugar
- Two cups of heavy cream
- One teaspoon of vanilla extract
- Half cup of unsweetened cocoa powder
- Half cup of white sugar
- Six egg yolk
- A pinch of salt
- Six egg whites
- One cup of whipped cream
- One cup of all-purpose flour

COOK TIME: 40 mins
SERVING: 12

INSTRUCTIONS

1. Take a large bowl.
2. Add the egg whites, and salt into a bowl.
3. Beat the egg whites well until they turn stiff.
4. Add the icing sugar, heavy cream, egg yolks and white sugar into the bowl.
5. Mix all the ingredients well to form a homogenous mixture.
6. Sift the flour and cocoa powder into a clean bowl.
7. Mix both the ingredients well.
8. Add the flour and cocoa powder slowly into the egg whites' mixture.
9. Fold the mixture well.
10. Preheat the oven at 180 degrees.
11. Take a greased baking tray.
12. Add the cake mixture into the tray.
13. Place the baking tray into the oven.
14. Bake the cake for forty minutes.
15. Dish out the cake when done.
16. Let the cake cool down.
17. Add the whipped cream on top of the cake.
18. Spread the cream all over the cake.
19. Now fold the cake slowly into a log
20. Your dish is ready to be served.

PARIS BREST

INGREDIENTS

- **For cake:**
- Half cup of butter
- One teaspoon of vanilla extract
- One teaspoon of white sugar
- Four whole egg
- A pinch of salt
- One cup of all-purpose flour
- **For filling:**
- Three tablespoons of icing sugar
- One cup of heavy cream
- Half cup of pastry cream
- Half teaspoon of vanilla extract

COOK TIME: 40 mins
SERVING: 12

INSTRUCTIONS

1. Take a large bowl.
2. Add the eggs and salt into a bowl.
3. Beat the eggs well until they turn stiff.
4. Add the sugar into the bowl.
5. Mix all the ingredients well to form a homogenous mixture.
6. Add the flour and vanilla extract into the bowl.
7. Mix both the ingredients well.
8. Fold the mixture well.
9. Preheat the oven at 180 degrees.
10. Take a greased baking dish.
11. Add the cake mixture into the dish.
12. Place the baking dish into the oven.
13. Bake the cake for forty minutes.
14. Dish out the cake when done.
15. Let the cake cool down.
16. Take a bowl.
17. Add the heavy cream, pastry cream, icing sugar and vanilla extract into the bowl.
18. Mix well.
19. Cut the cake in between.
20. Add the prepared icing on top of one of the cake piece.
21. Spread the cream all over the cake.
22. Now place the other pieces of cake on top of the icing.
23. Cut the cake into slices.
24. Your dish is ready to be served.

Tip: You can wrap the cake for about one month and easily freeze the cake.
25.

CROQUE MONSIEUR

INGREDIENTS

- Twelve ounces of ham
- One tablespoon of mustard mayo
- Four teaspoon of olive oil
- One teaspoon of dried oregano
- Two cloves of chopped garlic
- Sourdough bread slices
- One cup of gruyere cheese
- One teaspoon of salt
- One teaspoon of pepper
- **Béchamel sauce:**
- Four tablespoons of butter
- Two eggs
- Five tablespoons of flour
- Half cup of parmesan cheese
- A quarter teaspoon of nutmeg
- Three cups of milk
- Salt to taste
- Crushed black pepper to taste

COOK TIME: 30 mins
SERVING: 4

INSTRUCTIONS

1. Prepare the béchamel sauce in a sauce pan.
2. Add the butter, egg, milk, nutmeg, parmesan cheese, salt, crushed black pepper and all-purpose flour.
3. Cook the ingredients well.
4. Cook the béchamel sauce for about fifteen to twenty minutes.
5. Take a large pan.
6. Add the olive oil into the pan.
7. Add the chopped garlic into the pan.
8. Cook the garlic well.
9. Add the ham, dried oregano, salt and pepper into the pan as well.
10. Cook the ingredients well and then dish out.
11. Add the bread slices into the pan and toast them.
12. Add the ham mixture on one of the slices.
13. Add some of the gruyere cheese, mustard mayo and béchamel sauce on top.
14. Add another slice of bread on top.
15. The dish is ready to be served.

BRAISED DUCK WITH CHERRIES

INGREDIENTS

- Two tablespoons of butter
- One cup of chicken stock
- One tablespoon of cognac
- Two duck breasts cut into halves
- Half teaspoon of allspice berries
- Two bay leaf
- A pinch of salt
- A pinch of black pepper
- Half teaspoon of fennel seeds
- Half cup of red wine vinegar
- Half tablespoon of chopped ginger
- A quarter cup of turbinado sugar
- Two cups of cherries

COOK TIME: *30 mins*
SERVING: *2*

INSTRUCTIONS

1. Take a large pan.
2. Add the butter into the pan.
3. Add the duck breasts into the pan.
4. Cook the duck breast well.
5. Add the bay leaves, salt, black pepper, fennel seeds, cognac and allspice berries into the pan.
6. Cook the ingredients well.
7. Add the chopped garlic into the pan.
8. Add the ginger, red wine vinegar, cherries, turbinado sugar and chicken stock into the pan.
9. Cook the ingredients well.
10. Place a lid on top of the pan.
11. Cook the duck breasts for ten to fifteen minutes.
12. Dish out when the duck is done.
13. Your dish is ready to be served.

APPLE TART (BOUQUET DE ROSES)

INGREDIENTS

- Two cups of apple slices
- Half cup of icing sugar
- Two cups of sugar
- A pack of tart dough
- One cup of almond meal
- Half cup of lemon juice

COOK TIME: *30 mins*
SERVING: *4*

INSTRUCTIONS

1. Preheat the oven at 180 degrees.
2. Take a large bowl.
3. Add the almond meal and sugar into the bowl.
4. Lay the tart dough into greased tart dishes.
5. Cut the apple into thin slices.
6. Roll the slices and place on the tart dough.
7. Repeat this procedure for all the apple slices and place it on the tart dough.
8. Cover the dough with the apple rolls completely.
9. Add the almond meal mixture on top of apple slices.
10. Pour the lemon juice on top of the almond meal mixture.
11. Bake the dish properly for fifteen to twenty minutes.
12. Garnish the icing sugar on top of the tart.
13. The dish is ready to be served.

VEAL STEW

INGREDIENTS

- One and a half pound of veal pieces
- Six garlic cloves
- One bay leaf
- One tablespoon of chopped thyme
- One cup of chopped carrots
- A quarter cup of chopped leeks
- One cup of white wine
- Two cups of mushroom slices
- Two tablespoons of minced spring onion
- One cup of crème fraiche
- One tablespoon of chopped parsley
- One teaspoon of salt
- One tablespoon of black pepper
- A large sliced onion
- Three egg yolks
- A quarter cup of olive oil
- Half teaspoon of grated nutmeg
- One and a half cup of water

COOK TIME: *70 mins*
SERVING: *4*

INSTRUCTIONS

1. Take a large saucepan.
2. Add the olive oil into the pan.
3. Add the veal pieces into the pan.
4. Cook the veal pieces well and dish out when done.
5. Add the onions and garlic into the pan.
6. Cook well.
7. Add the celery into the pan.
8. Add the salt, nutmeg, egg yolk, crème fraiche, bay leaf, carrots, red pepper flakes, water, salt and black pepper into the pan.
9. Mix well.
10. Simmer the stew and add the white wine, veal pieces, leeks, mushroom and thyme for fifty minutes and then dish out.
11. Add the chopped parsley on top of the stew.
12. The dish is ready to be served.

Chapter 2: Traditional Champagne, Lorraine, and Alsace Recipes

Champagne is one of France's most momentous districts, flaunting a distinguished past in the realm of wine and French history. The food sources of Alsace Lorraine are probably viewed as the best food sources in France. The most famous foods used in these cities are Sauerkraut, pork, and juniper berries. You could be excused for assuming these food items as German food. These areas are located in northeastern France, which is the nearest to Germany. This is why there is a striking resemblance between the two cuisines. Following are some amazing recipes you need to follow:

ALSATIAN CHEESE TART

INGREDIENTS

- Half cup of cottage cheese
- A quarter teaspoon of salt
- Half cup of thinly sliced onion
- Half cup of sour cream
- Two tablespoons of grated parmesan cheese
- Two cups of chopped bacon
- Two tablespoons of olive oil
- Butter for greasing
- Black pepper to taste
- One pack of frozen pastry

COOK TIME: 30 *mins*
SERVING: 4

INSTRUCTIONS

1. Take a large pan.
2. Add the oil into the pan.
3. Add the onion slices into the pan.
4. Add the bacon, salt and black pepper into the pan.
5. Cook well and dish out the mixture.
6. Take a large bowl.
7. Add the sour cream and cheese into it.
8. Beat it properly.
9. Make it frothy.
10. Beat the mixture properly and then add the bacon mixture in the mixture.
11. Mix the mixture properly.
12. Lay the tart dough into greased tart dishes.
13. Bake the dish properly for ten to fifteen minutes.
14. Dish out when the tart turns golden brown in color.
15. Add the grated parmesan cheese on top.
16. The dish is ready to be served.

QUICHE LORRAINE

INGREDIENTS

- One tablespoon of olive oil
- A quarter cup of goat cheese
- One tablespoon of pumpkin seeds
- Half cup of chopped bacon
- Crushed black pepper to taste
- Four tablespoons of cream
- Two eggs
- Half teaspoon of freshly grated nutmeg
- Half teaspoon of salt
- **For dough:**
- Two cups of all-purpose flour
- Two teaspoons of fine sea salt
- Half cup of butter
- Two whole eggs
- A quarter cup of ice water

COOK TIME: *40 mins*
SERVING: *6*

INSTRUCTIONS

2. Take a large bowl.
3. Add the flour and sea salt into the bowl.
4. Mix the ingredients well and add the eggs, water and softened butter into the bowl.
5. Mix all the ingredients well to form a dough.
6. Take a large pan.
7. Add the olive oil into the pan.
8. Add the chopped bacon when the olive oil heats well.
9. Mix the onions and add the pumpkin seeds into the pan.
10. Cook the ingredients and then add the cream.
11. Switch off the heat.
12. Add the rest of the ingredients into the pan when it cools down.
13. Cook the ingredients for about five minutes.
14. Switch off the stove and let the mixture cool down.
15. Roll out the dough and lay half of it in a baking dish.
16. Add the cooked mixture on the dough.
17. Bake the quiche for about twenty to twenty-five minutes.
18. Dish out the quiche when it is done.
19. Your dish is ready to be served.

BUTTERMILK-SPINAC SPAETZLE

INGREDIENTS

- One and a half pound of baby spinach
- Six garlic cloves
- One bay leaf
- One tablespoon of chopped thyme
- One cup of buttermilk
- A quarter cup of chopped leeks
- One pack of frozen spaetzles
- One tablespoon of chopped parsley
- One teaspoon of salt
- One tablespoon of black pepper
- A large sliced onion
- A quarter cup of olive oil
- Half teaspoon of grated nutmeg
- One and a half cup of water

COOK TIME: *70 mins*
SERVING: *4*

INSTRUCTIONS

1. Take a large saucepan.
2. Add the olive oil into the pan.
3. Add the onions and garlic into the pan.
4. Cook well.
5. Add the baby spinach into the pan.
6. Add the salt, nutmeg, bay leaf, spaetzles, water, and black pepper into the pan.
7. Mix well.
8. Simmer the ingredients and add the buttermilk, leeks, and thyme for fifty minutes and then dish out.
9. Make sure all the water is dried properly.
10. Add the chopped parsley on top of the spaetzles.
11. The dish is ready to be served.

CHICKEN IN RIESLING WITH CABBAGE AND PRUNES

INGREDIENTS

- Two tablespoons of olive oil
- One cup of chopped shallots
- One cup of chopped carrots
- Half cup of chopped celery stalks
- One cup of chicken stock
- Half cup of thyme
- Half cup of rosemary
- Two cups of pitted prunes
- Two chicken breasts
- Two cups of green cabbage
- A pinch of salt
- A pinch of black pepper
- Half teaspoon of fennel seeds
- Half cup of red wine
- Half cup of Altasian riesling

COOK TIME: 30 mins
SERVING: 4

INSTRUCTIONS

1. Take a large pan.
2. Add the olive oil into the pan.
3. Add the chicken breasts into the pan.
4. Cook the chicken breast well.
5. Add the rosemary, thyme, Altasian Riesling, red wine and pitted prunes into the pan.
6. Cook the ingredients well.
7. Add the shallots and celery stalks into the pan.
8. Add the carrots, green cabbage and chicken stock into the pan.
9. Cook the ingredients well.
10. Place a lid on top of the pan.
11. Cook the chicken for ten to fifteen minutes.
12. Dish out when the chicken is done.
13. Your dish is ready to be served.

BOUDIN BLANC DE RETHEL

INGREDIENTS

- One and a half pound of pork sausages
- One pound of chicken thigh
- Two cups of cream
- One tablespoon of chopped thyme
- A quarter cup of brandy
- A quarter tablespoon of chopped garlic
- One tablespoon of chopped parsley
- One teaspoon of salt
- One tablespoon of black pepper

COOK TIME: 70 mins
SERVING: 4

INSTRUCTIONS

1. Take a large saucepan.
2. Add the olive oil into the pan.
3. Add the garlic into the pan.
4. Cook well.
5. Add the pork sausages and chicken thigh into the pan.
6. Add the salt, nutmeg, brandy, cream and black pepper into the pan.
7. Mix well.
8. Simmer the mixture and add the thyme and then dish out.
9. Add the chopped parsley on top of the ingredients.
10. The dish is ready to be served.

KIR ROYALE

INGREDIENTS

- One cup of dry champagne
- Two tablespoons of freshly chopped raspberries
- Four cups of sparkling water
- One cup of ice cubes
- Half cup of chambord

COOK TIME: *5 mins*
SERVING: *2*

INSTRUCTIONS

1. Take a blender.
2. Add the sparkling water, raspberries, dry champagne, chambord and ice cubes into the blender.
3. Blend everything well.
4. Pour the kir royale into glasses.
5. The dish is ready to be served.

Chapter 3: Traditional Normandy, and Brittany Recipes

How about we shut down the clichés! Brittany is more than crêpes and buckwheat hotcakes! Brittany's preferences incorporate the sea tang of shellfish, the deliciousness of crisp lord scallops, a bowl of shimmering juice, and buckwheat bourbon. With its wide scope of flavors from land and ocean, Breton cooking will make your mouth water. Numerous results of Normandy gastronomy are popular throughout the world: clams, lamb, juice, and clearly the camembert. You will definitely love the recipes below.

NORMANDY FRENCH ONION SOUP

INGREDIENTS

- Two cups of chicken stock
- Two crushed garlic
- A pinch of salt
- A pinch of black pepper
- Two tablespoons of olive oil
- One cup of dried white wine
- One cup of onion
- Three tablespoons of all-purpose flour
- Two tablespoons of Worcestershire sauce
- Three tablespoons of softened butter
- One bay leaf
- Two tablespoons of fresh thyme
- One cup of grated or sliced gruyere cheese
- French bread
- One cup of chopped dill

COOK TIME: *20 mins*
SERVING: *4*

INSTRUCTIONS

1. Take a large saucepan.
2. Add the oil and onions into the pan.
3. Cook the onions until they turn golden brown.
4. Add the crushed garlic into the pan.
5. Add the spices into the mixture.
6. Add the all-purpose flour, Worcestershire sauce and dried white wine.
7. Add the butter and then add the chicken stock.
8. Cover the pan with a lid for five minutes.
9. Let the soup cook properly.
10. Dish out the soup into soup bowls.
11. Add the grated or sliced cheese on top.
12. Bake the soup for ten minutes.
13. Switch off the oven when the cheese melts.
14. Add the chopped fresh dill on top.
15. Serve the soup with toasted bread slices.

The dish is ready to be served.

DUCK NORMANDY

INGREDIENTS

- Two tablespoons of olive oil
- Two teaspoons of chopped garlic
- One cup of sliced apples
- Two tablespoons of Dijon mustard
- Two tablespoons of apple cider vinegar
- Salt to taste
- Black pepper to taste
- Half cup of heavy cream
- Two tablespoons of chopped onions
- Two duck fillets
- A quarter cup of brandy
- One tablespoons of dried thyme

COOK TIME: *30 mins*
SERVING: *4*

INSTRUCTIONS

1. Take a pan.
2. Add the olive oil, and onions into the pan.
3. Cook the onions until they turn soft.
4. Add the minced garlic, duck pieces and apple slices into the pan.
5. Cook well.
6. Add the dried thyme, brandy, salt and black pepper into the pan.
7. Add the apple cider vinegar, heavy cream and Dijon mustard into the pan.
8. Cook the duck pieces for ten minutes.
9. Dish out when done.
10. Your dish is ready to be served.

NORMANDY PORK WITH PORK & CIDER

INGREDIENTS

- Two tablespoons of butter
- One tablespoon of cognac
- Two cups of pork pieces
- Half teaspoon of allspice
- Two tablespoons of Dijon mustard
- Two bay leaf
- A pinch of salt
- One cup of apple slices
- A pinch of black pepper
- Half cup of apple cider vinegar
- One cup of chopped onion
- Half tablespoon of chopped garlic and ginger

COOK TIME: 30 mins
SERVING: 4

INSTRUCTIONS

1. Take a large pan.
2. Add the butter into the pan.
3. Add the pork pieces into the pan.
4. Cook the pork pieces well.
5. Add the Dijon mustard, bay leaves, salt, black pepper, apple slices, cognac and allspice into the pan.
6. Cook the ingredients well.
7. Add the chopped garlic and ginger into the pan.
8. Add the apple cider vinegar into the pan.
9. Cook the ingredients well.
10. Place a lid on top of the pan.
11. Cook the pork pieces for ten to fifteen minutes.
12. Dish out when the pork is done.
13. Your dish is ready to be served.

BRITTANY CAKE

INGREDIENTS

- Half cup of butter
- Two cups of heavy cream
- One teaspoon of vanilla extract
- Two cups of all-purpose flour
- Half cup of white sugar
- Six egg yolks
- A pinch of salt
- One cup of fresh fruit compote

COOK TIME: *40 mins*
SERVING: *12*

INSTRUCTIONS

1. Take a large bowl.
2. Add the butter, heavy cream, egg yolks and white sugar into the bowl.
3. Mix all the ingredients well to form a homogenous mixture.
4. Add the flour, salt, vanilla extract and compote slowly into the egg yolks mixture.
5. Fold the mixture well.
6. Preheat the oven at 180 degrees.
7. Take a greased baking tray.
8. Add the cake mixture into the tray.
9. Place the baking tray into the oven.
10. Bake the cake for forty minutes.
11. Dish out the cake when done.
12. Your dish is ready to be served.

BRITTANY COOKIES

INGREDIENTS

- Half cup of salted butter
- Half cup of almond flour
- One teaspoon of vanilla extract
- Half cup of all-purpose flour
- Two egg yolks
- A pinch of salt
- A quarter cup of icing sugar

COOK TIME: 20 *mins*
SERVING: 6

INSTRUCTIONS

1. Take a large bowl.
2. Add the salted butter, almond flour, egg yolks and vanilla extract into the bowl.
3. Mix all the ingredients well to form a homogenous mixture.
4. Add the almond flour, all-purpose flour, and salt into mixture.
5. Fold the mixture well.
6. Preheat the oven at 180 degrees.
7. Take a greased baking tray.
8. Make the cookies using pipping bag on the tray.
9. Place the baking tray into the oven.
10. Bake the cookies for twenty minutes.
11. Dish out the cookies when done.
12. Your dish is ready to be served.

POULET A LA BRETONNE

INGREDIENTS

- Two tablespoons of olive oil
- Two teaspoons of chopped garlic
- One cup of sliced apples
- Four large chicken breast
- Two tablespoons of Dijon mustard
- Two tablespoons of apple cider vinegar
- Salt to taste
- Black pepper to taste
- Half cup of heavy cream
- Two tablespoons of chopped onions
- Four chicken fillets
- A quarter cup of brandy
- One tablespoons of dried thyme

INSTRUCTIONS

1. Take a pan.
2. Add the olive oil, and onions into the pan.
3. Cook the onions until they turn soft.
4. Add the minced garlic, chicken pieces and apple slices into the pan.
5. Cook well.
6. Add the dried thyme, brandy, salt and black pepper into the pan.
7. Add the apple cider vinegar, heavy cream and Dijon mustard into the pan.
8. Cook the chicken pieces for ten minutes.
9. Dish out when done.
10. Your dish is ready to be served.

COOK TIME: *20 mins*
SERVING: *4*

Chapter 4: Traditional Loire Valley and Central France Recipes

The Loire Valley impeccably addresses a sweet lifestyle with a pleasant climate, delectable food, flavorful wine, and well-disposed individuals. Supposedly the core of the French food was created in the illustrious kitchens of the Loire valley. Along your way in the Loire Valley, you will unavoidably see the numerous heavenly connoisseur treats of the Loire locale, well prepared and introduced. The Center locale of France is a paradise for experts and admirers of French country food. Follow the recipes below to indulge in the flavors of these two cities.

CHEESECAKE RECIPE FROM LORRIE VALLEY

INGREDIENTS

- Two cups of cream cheese
- One tablespoon of vanilla essence
- One cup of strawberries
- One pack of semi crushed ginger bread
- Half cup of soft cheese
- Three whole eggs
- Half cup of melted butter
- Half cup of caster sugar

COOK TIME: 20 mins
SERVING: 4

INSTRUCTIONS

1. Take a mixing bowl.
2. Add the cream cheese, cheese, sugar, and egg into the bowl.
3. Mix well until the mixture turns light and fluffy.
4. Add the vanilla essence and strawberries into the mixture.
5. Mix well.
6. Take a baking dish.
7. Add the butter and crushed ginger bread in the bottom of the dish and press the mixture well.
8. Pour the cheese mixture on top of the biscuit crust.
9. Place the dish in the oven for about twenty minutes.
10. Dish out when the cheese cake turns golden brown in color.
11. Your dish is ready to be served.

Tip: You can add lemon zest into the cheese mixture for a zesty flavor.

LORRIE VALLEY PORK RILLETTES

INGREDIENTS

- Two tablespoons of butter
- One tablespoon of dried thyme
- Two cups of pork mince
- Half teaspoon of allspice
- Two bay leaf
- A pinch of salt
- A pinch of white pepper
- Two tablespoons of brandy
- One cup of chopped shallots
- Toasted bread slices for serving

COOK TIME: 30 *mins*
SERVING: 4

INSTRUCTIONS

1. Take a large pan.
2. Add the butter into the pan.
3. Add the pork mince into the pan.
4. Cook the pork mince well.
5. Add the brandy, bay leaves, salt, white pepper, and allspice into the pan.
6. Cook the ingredients well.
7. Add the shallots and dried thyme into the pan.
8. Cook the ingredients well.
9. Place a lid on top of the pan.
10. Cook the pork for ten to fifteen minutes.
11. Dish out when the pork is done and serve it with toasted bread.
12. Your dish is ready to be served.

CHARD ROASTED SALMON WITH FENNEL SALAD

INGREDIENTS

- Half fennel bulb
- Two tablespoons of olive oil
- One tablespoon of dried thyme
- Two tablespoons of orange juice
- Half teaspoon of anchovy paste
- One pound of salmon fillet
- A pinch of salt
- A pinch of black pepper
- Two tablespoons of chopped chard leaves

COOK TIME: *30 mins*
SERVING: *4*

INSTRUCTIONS

1. Take a large pan.
2. Add the olive oil into the pan.
3. Add the salmon fillet into the pan.
4. Cook the salmon well.
5. Add the salt and black pepper into the pan.
6. Cook the salmon well and dish out when done.
7. Take a bowl.
8. Add the chopped chard leaves, anchovy paste, fennel bulb, orange juice and dried thyme into the bowl.
9. Mix the ingredients well.
10. Serve the salad with the salmon filet.
11. Your dish is ready to be served.

BUCKWHEAT CREPES WITH CREAMY LEEKS AND BAKED EGGS

INGREDIENTS

- Two tablespoons of creamy softened butter
- One cup of buckwheat flour
- Two tablespoons of milk
- Two large eggs
- One teaspoon of vanilla extract
- One cup of chopped leeks
- A quarter cup of cream cheese
- Three eggs
- Salt to taste

COOK TIME: 25 *mins*
SERVING: 3

INSTRUCTIONS

1. Take a bowl.
2. Add the creamy softened butter into the bowl.
3. Add in the buckwheat flour, milk, vanilla extract, and eggs.
4. Mix the ingredients carefully.
5. Add the mixture in small quantities in a pan and spread in the form of crepes.
6. Let the crepes turn golden on both sides.
7. Dish out the crepes when done.
8. Take a bowl.
9. Add the cream cheese, salt, leeks and eggs into the bowl.
10. Mix the ingredients well.
11. Fold the cooked crepes into a box.
12. Add the egg mixture into the crepe boxes.
13. Bake the crepes for ten minutes.
14. Dish out.
15. Your dish is ready to be served.

LUDO LEFEBVRE'S OMELET

INGREDIENTS

- Two tablespoons of butter
- Half cup of heavy cream
- A pinch of salt
- A pinch of black pepper
- Two tablespoons of chopped fresh chives
- Four eggs
- One red onions
- French bread slices

COOK TIME: *15 mins*
SERVING: *2*

INSTRUCTIONS

1. Take a bowl.
2. Add the red onions, eggs, salt, black pepper, and chives into the bowl.
3. Mix the ingredients well.
4. Take a large pan.
5. Add the butter and let it meltdown.
6. Add in the egg mixture.
7. Cook the eggs until they turn light golden in color.
8. Dish out when the eggs are done.
9. Add the heavy cream on top.
10. Your dish is ready to be served.

THE LOFFTIEST SOUFFLE

INGREDIENTS

- Eight eggs
- Four drops of lemon juice
- Two cups of milk
- A pinch of salt
- Three tablespoons of all-purpose flour
- Five ounces of gruyere cheese
- Half cup of flour
- Five tablespoons of butter

COOK TIME: *40 mins*
SERVING: *6*

INSTRUCTIONS

1. Take a large bowl.
2. Add the milk, eggs, lemon juice, salt, all-purpose flour, gruyere cheese, flour and butter into the bowl.
3. Mix all the ingredients well.
4. Pour the mixture into a baking dish.
5. Bake the dish for twenty minutes.
6. Your dish is ready to be served.

Chapter 5: Traditional Burgundy and Franche-Comté Recipes

The Franche-Comté food is made of cheddar and charcuterie, for certain varieties depending on the division. Consequently, in the Jura, numerous recipes include yellow wine. Generally speaking, the conventional plans of the Franche-Comté are more caloric because of the greasy sauces in them. Burgundy is answerable for a portion of France's most commended dishes. The culinary experts, ranchers, and ordinary residents of Burgundy love pretty much everything in food and wine. We will try some of the recipes belonging to these regions below.

GASTON GERARD CH8CKEN

INGREDIENTS

- Two tablespoons of olive oil
- Four large chicken thighs
- Two tablespoons of Dijon mustard
- One cup of white wine
- Salt to taste
- Black pepper to taste
- Half cup of heavy cream
- Half cup of Swiss cheese
- A quarter cup of brandy
- One tablespoons of dried thyme

COOK TIME: 30 mins
SERVING: 4

INSTRUCTIONS

1. Take a pan.
2. Add the olive oil into the pan.
3. Add the chicken pieces and thyme into the pan.
4. Cook well.
5. Add the heavy cream, brandy, salt and black pepper into the pan.
6. Add the white wine, Swiss cheese and Dijon mustard into the pan.
7. Cook the chicken pieces for ten minutes.
8. Dish out when done.
9. Your dish is ready to be served.

POULET A LA COMTOISE

INGREDIENTS

- Two tablespoons of olive oil
- One cup of crème fraiche
- Salt to taste
- Black pepper to taste
- Half cup of parmesan cheese
- Two tablespoons of chopped shallots
- Two chicken fillets
- A quarter cup of brandy
- One cup of mushroom slices

COOK TIME: *30 mins*
SERVING: *4*

INSTRUCTIONS

1. Take a pan.
2. Add the olive oil, and shallots into the pan.
3. Cook the shallots until they turn soft.
4. Add the chicken pieces into the pan.
5. Cook well.
6. Add the mushroom slices, brandy, salt and black pepper into the pan.
7. Add the crème fraiche into the pan.
8. Cook the chicken pieces for ten minutes.
9. Dish out when done.
10. Garnish the dish with parmesan cheese on top.
11. Your dish is ready to be served.

BREADED COMTE BITES WITH ESPELLETE PEPPER CREAM

INGREDIENTS

- Two tablespoons of olive oil
- One cup of diced comte
- Four large pastry sheets
- Two cups of crème fraiche
- Salt to taste
- Black pepper to taste
- Two tablespoons of chopped onions
- Half cup of chopped chives
- One teaspoon of espelette pepper

COOK TIME: 30 mins
SERVING: 4

INSTRUCTIONS

1. Take a pan.
2. Add the olive oil, and onions into the pan.
3. Cook the onions until they turn soft.
4. Add the chopped chives into the pan.
5. Cook well and dish out.
6. Cut the pastry sheets in half.
7. Stuff the formed mixture and diced comte on the pastry sheets.
8. Roll the pasty sheets and close the open ends with a fork
9. Place the pastries on a greased baking dish.
10. Bake the pastries for thirty minutes.
11. Dish out when the pastries turn golden brown in color.
12. Take a bowl.
13. Add the crème fraiche, salt, black pepper and espelette pepper into the bowl.
14. Mix well and serve the dip with the pastries
15. Your dish is ready to be served.

DIJON GINGERBREAD

INGREDIENTS

- One teaspoon of mustard powder
- Two tablespoons of mixed ginger spice
- One cup of brown sugar
- Ten tablespoons of unsalted butter
- One teaspoon of vanilla extract
- Half cup of molasses
- Half cup of water
- One egg
- One teaspoon of baking soda
- Two cups of all-purpose flour
- One cup of rye flour

INSTRUCTIONS

1. Take a large bowl.
2. Add the mustard powder, unsalted butter, mixed ginger spice, brown sugar, vanilla extract, baking soda, all-purpose flour, rye flour, egg and water into the bowl.
3. Mix them well to form a dough.
4. Roll out the dough into a semi-thick sheet with the help of flour.
5. Cut out round shapes with the help of a shape cutter from the dough.
6. Take a greased baking tray.
7. Place the round shapes of dough on the tray.
8. Bake the gingerbread shapes for twenty minutes and then dish out.
9. Your gingerbread is ready to be served.

COOK TIME: 10 mins
SERVING: 4

DIJON PEAR SALAD

INGREDIENTS

- Three cups of arugula leaves
- One cup of pear slices
- Half cup of fresh thyme
- Half teaspoon of smoked paprika
- Two tablespoons minced garlic
- Half cup of chopped celery
- Two tablespoons of olive oil
- Two tablespoons of honey
- Half cup of Dijon mustard

COOK TIME: 0 mins
SERVING: 2

INSTRUCTIONS

1. Take a large bowl.
2. Add the honey, Dijon mustard, olive oil, paprika and garlic into a bowl.
3. Mix all the ingredients well to form a homogenous mixture.
4. Add the pear slices, arugula leaves, fresh thyme and chopped celery on top of the mixture.
5. Toss the salad to make sure everything is mixed properly.
6. Your dish is ready to be served.

DIJON NONNETTES

INGREDIENTS

- One cup of black currant or black berry jam
- One teaspoon of mustard powder
- Two tablespoons of mixed ginger spice
- One cup of brown sugar
- Ten tablespoons of unsalted butter
- One teaspoon of vanilla extract
- Half cup of molasses
- Half cup of water
- One egg
- One teaspoon of baking soda
- Two cups of all-purpose flour
- One cup of rye flour

COOK TIME: *10 mins*
SERVING: *4*

INSTRUCTIONS

1. Take a large bowl.
2. Add the mustard powder, unsalted butter, mixed ginger spice, brown sugar, vanilla extract, baking soda, all-purpose flour, rye flour, egg and water into the bowl.
3. Mix them well to form a dough.
4. Roll out the dough into a semi-thick sheet with the help of flour.
5. Cut out round shapes with the help of a shape cutter from the dough.
6. Add the jam on the round shapes.
7. Cover the jam with the dough to form a ball.
8. Take a greased baking tray.
9. Place the balls of dough on the tray.
10. Bake the nonnettes for twenty minutes and then dish out.
11. Your dish is ready to be served.

Chapter 6: Traditional Bordeaux, Périgord, Gascony, and Basque country Recipes

This region has somewhere around 5,000 remarkably styled gothic-rococo-roused structures that depict the area's rich recorded foundation. They have so many exhibition halls. Individuals in this space are extremely energetic about workmanship and wine. This region has the longest realized shopping strip in Europe. Special kinds of black and dark red grapes are found in the locale of Bordeaux, considering the development of novel and refined wines. As locales that are intensely ranch-based, they likewise offer top-notch sheep, chicken, pigeon, capon, and duck. The most famous food is foie gras in this region. Following are some more delicious recipes that you will love trying!

BASQUE POTATO AND PEPPER TORTILLA WITH HAM AND CHEESE

INGREDIENTS

- Half cup of melted butter
- Two cups of sliced potatoes
- Two cups of sliced onions
- Two cups of ham slices
- Two tablespoons of cayenne pepper
- A pinch of salt
- One cup of gruyere cheese slices
- A pinch of freshly crushed black pepper
- Four whole eggs
- One cup of red bell pepper slices

COOK TIME: 30 mins
SERVING: 4

INSTRUCTIONS

1. Take a large pan.
2. Add the butter into the pan and melt it.
3. Add the potatoes, ham, red bell peppers, onions, salt and pepper into the pan.
4. Cook the potatoes well and then add the cayenne pepper into the pan.
5. Cook the dish for two to three minutes and then dish out.
6. Add the eggs when the mixture cools down.
7. Mix everything well.
8. Add the formed mixture into a greased baking dish.
9. Place the baking dish in a preheated oven.
10. Bake the tortilla for about twenty minutes.
11. Dish out the tortilla when it attains a golden brown color.
12. The dish is ready to be served.

Tip: You can use olive oil instead of butter in this recipe.

BASQUE CHERRY PIE

INGREDIENTS

- One cup of cherry preserves
- **For dough:**
- Two cups of all-purpose flour
- Two teaspoons of fine sea salt
- Half cup of unsalted soft butter
- Two whole egg
- A quarter cup of ice water

COOK TIME: *40 mins*
SERVING: *6*

INSTRUCTIONS

1. Take a large bowl.
2. Add the flour and sea salt into the bowl.
3. Mix the ingredients well and add the eggs, water and softened butter into the bowl.
4. Mix all the ingredients well to form a dough.
5. Roll out the dough and lay half of it in a round baking dish.
6. Add the cherry preserves on the dough and cover the mixture with rest of the dough.
7. Bake the pie for about twenty to twenty five minutes.
8. Dish out the pie when it is done.
9. Your dish is ready to be served.

BAYONNE HAM OMELET

INGREDIENTS

- Two tablespoons of butter
- Half cup of chopped bayonne ham slices
- A pinch of salt
- A pinch of black pepper
- Two tablespoons of chopped fresh chives
- Four eggs
- One red onions

COOK TIME: *15 mins*
SERVING: *2*

INSTRUCTIONS

1. Take a bowl.
2. Add the chopped bayonne ham, red onions, eggs, salt, black pepper, and chives into the bowl.
3. Mix the ingredients well.
4. Take a large pan.
5. Add the butter and let it meltdown.
6. Add in the egg mixture.
7. Cook the eggs until they turn light golden in color.
8. Dish out when the eggs are done.
9. Your dish is ready to be served.

POULET AU POT WITH GROSS SEL SAUCE

INGREDIENTS

- One cup of chicken pieces
- One tablespoon of kosher salt
- One tablespoon of black pepper
- Two cups of red wine
- Two tablespoons of olive oil
- One bay leaf
- One teaspoon of sugar
- Two thyme sprigs
- Half cup of diced bacon
- One cup of carrots
- One cup of mushrooms
- One onions
- One tablespoon of flour
- Two tablespoons of brandy
- One teaspoon of chopped garlic
- Half cup of gros gel sauce
- Parsley for garnishing

COOK TIME: *20 mins*
SERVING: *2*

INSTRUCTIONS

1. Take a large bowl.
2. Add the chicken pieces into it.
3. Season the chicken with pepper and salt.
4. Combine the chicken with gros gel sauce, red wine, bay leaf and thyme.
5. Cover it and marinate for thirty minutes.
6. Cook the bacons until they become crispy.
7. Add the marinated chicken into it.
8. Cook it until the chicken becomes golden brown.
9. Add the onions, carrots, tomato paste and the button mushrooms into the pan.
10. Add the garlic, and all-purpose flour into the pan.
11. Cook well until the flour turns fragrant.
12. Add the brandy into the mixture.
13. Cook the dish for five more minutes and then dish out.
14. Add the chopped parsley on top and serve hot.

FRENCH TOMATO TART

INGREDIENTS

- One tablespoon of olive oil
- A quarter cup of blue cheese
- One cup of chopped tomatoes
- Crushed black pepper to taste
- Four teaspoons of sugar
- Half teaspoon of freshly grated nutmeg
- Salt to taste
- **For dough:**
- Two cups of all-purpose flour
- Two teaspoons of fine sea salt
- Half cup of unsalted soft butter
- Two whole egg
- A quarter cup of ice water

COOK TIME: 40 mins
SERVING: 6

INSTRUCTIONS

1. Take a large bowl.
2. Add the flour and sea salt into the bowl.
3. Mix the ingredients well and add the eggs, water and softened butter into the bowl.
4. Mix all the ingredients well to form a dough.
5. Take a large pan.
6. Add the olive oil into the pan.
7. Add the tomatoes when the olive oil heats well.
8. Mix the tomatoes and add the sugar into the pan.
9. Cook the ingredients until the sugar is melted.
10. Add the black pepper, salt, freshly grated nutmeg and blue cheese into the pan.
11. Cook the ingredients for about five minutes.
12. Switch off the stove and let the mixture cool down.
13. Roll out the dough and lay half of it in a tart baking dish.
14. Add the cooked mixture on the dough.
15. Bake the tart for about twenty to twenty five minutes.
16. Dish out the tart when it is done.
17. Your dish is ready to be served.

PRUNE FLAN

INGREDIENTS

- **For dough:**
- Two and a quarter teaspoons of active yeast
- One cup of water
- Two and a half cups of all-purpose flour
- One teaspoon of sugar
- Two tablespoons of olive oil
- One tablespoon of sea salt
- **For custard mixture:**
- Three eggs
- Two cups cream
- One teaspoon of vanilla extract
- Two tablespoons of caster sugar
- One tablespoon of brandy
- Two tablespoons of corn flour
- Two tbsp. of orange essence
- Two cups of chopped prunes

COOK TIME: *20 mins*
SERVING: *4*

INSTRUCTIONS

2. Take a mixing bowl.
3. Add the all-purpose flour, sugar, active yeast and sea salt into the bowl.
4. Mix well and then add the olive oil and water into the bowl.
5. Knead the dough well and place it aside for thirty to forty minutes.
6. Roll out the ball of dough into semi thick sheets.
7. Take a bowl.
8. Add the eggs, cream, vanilla extract, caster sugar, brandy, orange essence, corn flour, brandy and chopped prunes.
9. Mix well
10. Line the dough in a greased dish.
11. Pour the egg mixture on the rolled dough.
12. Preheat the oven at 180 degrees.
13. Place the flan on a greased and lined up baking tray.
14. Bake the flan for twenty to thirty minutes or until it turns golden brown.
15. Dish out when done.
16. Your dish is ready to be served.

PASCAL AUSSIGNAC LE FAMEUX CASSOULET

INGREDIENTS

- One cup of plain beans
- One teaspoon of kosher salt
- Half pound of mushrooms
- Two cups of black quinoa
- One cup of broad beans
- One teaspoon of black pepper
- Parsley for garnishing
- One teaspoon of garlic powder
- Two celery stalks
- Two tablespoons of olive oil
- One cup of rocket cress
- Two tablespoons of apple cider vinegar
- One cup of chopped tomatoes

COOK TIME: 35 mins
SERVING: 5

INSTRUCTIONS

2. Take a large bowl.
3. Add the plain and broad beans in water.
4. Add the salt in the beans.
5. Heat the olive oil.
6. Add the mushrooms, beans, quinoa and cook it until becomes brown.
7. Season the mixture with black pepper.
8. Add the garlic powder and rocket cress and cook it well.
9. Add the celery stalks and tomatoes into the mixture.
10. Cook the beans along with all the ingredients for forty five minutes.
11. Add the apple cider vinegar into the pan and mix well.
12. Dish out the cassoulet.
13. Add the chopped parsley on top.
14. Your dish is ready to be served.

BAKED WHOLE TRUFFLES IN SALT

INGREDIENTS

- One cup of pork fat slices
- One pound of whole truffles
- Two teaspoons of minced garlic
- Four egg whites
- Salt to taste
- Black pepper

COOK TIME: 45 mins
SERVING: 4

INSTRUCTIONS

1. Preheat the oven at 180 degrees.
2. Take a bowl.
3. Add the pork fat slices, whole truffles, minced garlic, egg whites, salt and black pepper into the bowl.
4. Mix all the ingredients well.
5. Add the mixture into a greased baking dish.
6. Bake the truffles for forty five minutes.
7. Dish out the truffles when done.
8. Crack open the shell.
9. Your dish is ready to be served.

BALLOTINE DE POULET

INGREDIENTS

- Two tablespoons of olive oil
- Two teaspoons of chopped garlic
- One cup of chopped bacon
- One cup of spinach
- Two tablespoons of chopped fresh herbs
- Salt to taste
- Black pepper to taste
- Two tablespoons of chopped onions
- Thinly sliced chicken breast
- Half cup of cheese sauce

COOK TIME: 30 *mins*
SERVING: 4

INSTRUCTIONS

1. Preheat the oven at 180 degrees.
2. Take a pan.
3. Add the chopped bacon, spinach, chopped garlic, olive oil, and onions in the pan.
4. Mix well.
5. Season the mixture with salt and black pepper.
6. Add the cooked mixture on the chicken slices and fold the slices to form a roll.
7. Place the chicken rolls on a greased baking pan.
8. Drizzle cheese sauce on top.
9. Bake the chicken rolls for thirty minutes.
10. Dish out when done.
11. Your dish is ready to be served.

CAP FERRET OYSTERS

INGREDIENTS

- A quarter cup of red wine
- One pound of boiled ferret oysters
- Two teaspoons of minced shallots
- Two tablespoons of lemon juice
- Two tablespoons of chopped fresh mint leaves
- Salt to taste
- Black pepper

COOK TIME: *5 mins*
SERVING: *4*

INSTRUCTIONS

1. Take a bowl.
2. Add the red wine, oysters, minced shallots, lemon juice, mint leaves, salt and black pepper into the bowl.
3. Microwave the ingredients for five minutes.
4. Mix all the ingredients well.
5. Add the mixture into a serving dish.
6. Your dish is ready to be served.

Chapter 7: Traditional Provence-Alpes-Côte d'Azur Recipes

Located on the southern side of France, Provence-Côte d'Azur offers huge areas of rich blue Mediterranean shoreline and tasty daylight food. Bouillabaisse is known as the mark dish of this area. Provençal food is fixated on various kinds of local spices like garlic and olive oil. Their splendor hoists the meats, vegetables, and fish. Such blends bring about satisfyingly rich and bright rarities saturated with provincial characters.

FRENCH BOUILLABAISE

INGREDIENTS

- Two strips of orange peel
- Three bay leaves
- One cup of chopped onions
- One tablespoon of black pepper
- One cup of chopped leek
- Two tablespoons of olive oil
- Eight dried chilies
- Two teaspoons of chopped garlic
- One cup of mussels
- One cup of mixed Mediterranean fish
- One cup of tomato paste
- A pinch of saffron
- One teaspoon of black pepper
- Two cups of ripe tomatoes
- Two cups of fish stock
- Two tablespoons of pernod
- One Star anise
- A pinch of salt
- One tablespoon of chopped fresh chives

COOK TIME: *20 mins*
SERVING: *4*

INSTRUCTIONS

1. Take a large pan.
2. Add the oil and onions into the pan.
3. Cook the onions until they turn soft and translucent.
4. Add the garlic into the pan.
5. Cook the mixture well.
6. Add the tomato paste, chopped ripe tomatoes and spices.
7. Cook the mixture for five minutes.
8. Add the mussels, and Mediterranean fish into the pan.
9. Cook the ingredients well.
10. Add the fish stock, chopped leeks, dried chilies, pernod and orange peel.
11. Cover the pan and cook for ten minutes.
12. Garnish the dish with chopped fresh chives.
13. Your dish is ready to be served.

FRENCH PASTIS

INGREDIENTS

- One cup of pernod
- Four cups of sparkling water
- One cup of ice cubes

COOK TIME: *0 mins*
SERVING: *2*

INSTRUCTIONS

1. Take a blender.
2. Add the sparkling water, pernod and ice cubes into the blender.
3. Blend everything well.
4. Pour the pastis into glasses.
   The dish is ready to be served.

FRENCH DAUBE

INGREDIENTS

- Two strips of thyme leaves
- Two cups of boiled noodles
- One cup of chopped onions
- One tablespoon of black pepper
- One cup of chopped leek
- Two tablespoons of olive oil
- Two teaspoons of chopped garlic
- One cup of chopped carrots
- One cup of beef
- One cup of tomato paste
- A pinch of rosemary
- One teaspoon of black pepper
- Two ripe tomato
- Two cups of beef stock
- One cup of red wine
- A pinch of salt
- One tablespoon of chopped fresh chives

COOK TIME: 40 mins
SERVING: 4

INSTRUCTIONS

1. Take a large pan.
2. Add the oil and onions into the pan.
3. Cook the onions until they turn soft and translucent.
4. Add the garlic into the pan.
5. Cook the mixture well.
6. Add the tomato paste, black pepper, chopped ripe tomatoes and red wine.
7. Cook the mixture for five minutes.
8. Add the beef chunks, salt, rosemary, carrots and thyme into the pan.
9. Cook the ingredients well.
10. Add the beef stock, and chopped leeks into the pan.
11. Cover the pan and cook for twenty minutes.
12. Garnish the dish with chopped fresh chives.
13. Your dish is ready to be served.

FRENCH TAPENADE

INGREDIENTS

- One teaspoon of chopped capers
- Three tablespoons of minced garlic
- One cup of black olives
- Two tablespoons of anchovy paste
- One teaspoon of salt
- Two tablespoons of parsley
- A quarter cup of olive oil
- Two tablespoons of lime juice
- A quarter cup of fresh oregano
- Black pepper to taste
- Toasted bread for serving

COOK TIME: *90 mins*
SERVING: *4*

INSTRUCTIONS

1. Heat the water in a stockpot over medium-high heat.
2. Add the olives into the pot.
3. Cook for fifty to sixty minutes, or until the olives are tender.
4. Add the olives into a blender once done.
5. Add the parsley, lime juice, fresh oregano, minced garlic, anchovy paste, capers, salt, mint, olive oil, and black pepper into the blender.
6. Blend everything well and dish out in a bowl.
7. Your dish is ready to be served with toasted bread on the side.

FRENCH NOUGAT

INGREDIENTS

- Two cups of organic sugar
- One cup of pistachios
- Two cups of peanuts
- Two cups of organic light syrup
- Two egg whites
- Two tablespoons of glucose syrup
- One cup of water

INSTRUCTIONS

1. Take a large pot.
2. Add the organic sugar, light syrup, glucose syrup, peanuts, egg whites, water and pistachios into the pot.
3. Cook all the ingredients well until the mixture starts turning thick.
4. Pour the mixture into a dish.
5. Let the mixture cool down.
6. Cut into bite size pieces.
   Your dish is ready to be served.

COOK TIME: *25 mins*
SERVING: *4*

OMELETTE AUX TRUFFLES

INGREDIENTS

- Two tablespoons of butter
- Half cup of chopped truffles
- A pinch of salt
- A pinch of black pepper
- Two tablespoons of chopped fresh thyme
- Four eggs
- Chopped fresh parsley for serving

COOK TIME: 15 mins
SERVING: 2

INSTRUCTIONS

1. Take a bowl.
2. Add the chopped truffles, eggs, salt, black pepper, and thyme into the bowl.
3. Mix the ingredients well.
4. Take a large pan.
5. Add the butter and let it meltdown.
6. Add in the egg mixture.
7. Cook the eggs until they turn light golden in color.
8. Dish out when the eggs are done.
9. Add the chopped parsley on top. Your dish is ready to be served.

FRENCH RATATOUILLE

INGREDIENTS

- Kosher salt to taste
- Black pepper to taste
- One cup of eggplant pieces
- One cup of zucchini pieces
- A quarter cup of chopped marjoram dates
- One cup of chopped chives
- One cup of cherry tomatoes
- Half cup of summer savory sprigs
- Two tablespoons of minced garlic
- Two tablespoons of dried thyme
- Half cup of chopped parsley
- Two teaspoons of Herbs de Provence
- Half cup of chopped onion
- Two tablespoons of olive oil
- Half cup of basil leaves
- One cup of red bell pepper
- One tablespoon of crushed red pepper
- One bay leaf
- Half teaspoon of fennel leaves

COOK TIME: *30 mins*
SERVING: *4*

INSTRUCTIONS

1. Preheat the oven at 150 degrees.
2. Take a large pan.
3. Add the olive oil and chopped onions into it.
4. Cook the onions until they turn light brown in color.
5. Add the minced garlic into the pan.
6. Cook the mixture for five minutes.
7. Season the mixture with salt and pepper.
8. Add the spices and all the vegetables.
9. Crush the cherry tomatoes in a bowl and add the salt.
10. Dish the mixture out in a plate when the vegetables are done.
11. Add the crushed tomatoes into the pan.
12. Cook the tomatoes for ten minutes or until they turn soft.
13. Add the vegetable pieces one by one and form a design into a baking pan.
14. Pour the tomato mixture on top.
15. Add the chopped marjoram dates, basil and parsley leaves on top and bake the mixture for ten to fifteen minutes.
16. Dish out when done.
17. Your dish is ready to be served.

FRENCH AIOLI

INGREDIENTS

- Two egg yolks
- One and a half cup of lemon juice
- A pinch of kosher salt
- A quarter cup of olive oil
- Two tablespoons of minced garlic
- Half teaspoon of Dijon mustard
- Black pepper to taste

COOK TIME: *15 mins*
SERVING: *4*

INSTRUCTIONS

1. Take a pan.
2. Add the olive oil and minced garlic into the pan.
3. Cook the garlic well.
4. Add the Dijon mustard, black pepper, kosher salt, lemon juice and egg yolks into the pan.
5. Cook all the ingredients well.
6. Continue mixing until the sauce turns thick.
7. Dish out when done.
8. Your dish is ready to be served.

TARTE TROPEZIENNE

INGREDIENTS

- **For the bread:**
- One cup of butter
- One teaspoon of vanilla extract
- One teaspoon of white sugar
- Four whole egg
- Half cup of milk
- A pinch of salt
- One teaspoon of yeast
- Four cups of all-purpose flour
- **For filling:**
- Three tablespoons of icing sugar
- One cup of heavy cream
- Half cup of pastry cream
- Half teaspoon of vanilla extract

COOK TIME: 40 mins
SERVING: 12

INSTRUCTIONS

1. Take a large bowl.
2. Add the eggs, yeast, all-purpose flour, sugar, vanilla extract, butter and salt into the bowl.
3. Knead the mixture well to form a dough.
4. Preheat the oven at 180 degrees.
5. Take a greased baking dish.
6. Add the dough mixture into the dish.
7. Place the baking dish into the oven.
8. Bake the dough for forty minutes.
9. Dish out the bread when done.
10. Let the cake cool down.
11. Take a bowl.
12. Add the heavy cream, pastry cream, icing sugar and vanilla extract into the bowl.
13. Mix well.
14. Cut the bread in between.
15. Add the prepared icing on top of one of the bread piece.
16. Spread the cream all over the bread.
17. Now place the other piece of bread on top of the icing.
18. Your dish is ready to be served.

FROMAGE DE CHEVRE

INGREDIENTS

- One tablespoon of olive oil
- A quarter cup of goat cheese
- One tablespoon of milk
- Two cups of fresh chopped spinach
- Crushed black pepper to taste
- Four eggs
- Half teaspoon of freshly grated nutmeg
- Salt to taste
- **For dough:**
- Two cups of all-purpose flour
- Two teaspoons of fine sea salt
- Half cup of unsalted soft butter
- Two whole egg
- A quarter cup of ice water

COOK TIME: *40 mins*
SERVING: *6*

INSTRUCTIONS

1. Take a large bowl.
2. Add the flour and sea salt into the bowl.
3. Mix the ingredients well and add the eggs, water and softened butter into the bowl.
4. Mix all the ingredients well to form a dough.
5. Take a large pan.
6. Add the olive oil into the pan.
7. Add the eggs when the olive oil heats well.
8. Mix the eggs and add the chopped spinach into the pan.
9. Cook the ingredients until the spinach is wilted.
10. Add the milk, black pepper, salt, freshly grated nutmeg and goat cheese into the pan.
11. Cook the ingredients for about five minutes.
12. Switch off the stove and let the mixture cool down.
13. Roll out the dough and lay half of it in a round baking dish.
14. Add the cooked mixture on the dough and cover the mixture with rest of the dough.
15. Bake the pie for about twenty to twenty five minutes.
16. Dish out the pie when it is done.
17. Your dish is ready to be served.

Chapter 8: Traditional Corsica Recipes

Finding the food of Corsica implies going on an outing for realness and custom. Different customs and recipe plans have always been passed on to the next generation. Prisuttu, heavenly lean ham from pigs raised on oak seeds or chestnuts, is a must in Corsica. Chestnut polenta is always served with pig stew. Corsican cuisine is real and liberal food that you need to try!

BROCCIU CHEESE AND MINT OMELET

INGREDIENTS

- Two tablespoons of butter
- Half cup of chopped mint leaves
- A pinch of salt
- A pinch of black pepper
- Half cup of grated brocciu or goat cheese
- Four eggs

COOK TIME: *15 mins*
SERVING: *2*

INSTRUCTIONS

1. Take a bowl.
2. Add the chopped mint leaves, eggs, salt, black pepper, and grated cheese into the bowl.
3. Mix the ingredients well.
4. Take a large pan.
5. Add the butter and let it meltdown.
6. Add in the egg mixture.
7. Cook the eggs until they turn light golden in color.
8. Dish out the omelet when done.
9. Your dish is ready to be served.

CORSICAN MINESTRA

INGREDIENTS

- Four cups of vegetable stock
- Two tablespoons of crushed garlic
- Salt to taste
- Black pepper to taste
- Two tablespoons of olive oil
- One cup of dried white wine
- One cup of onion
- One cup of mixed greens
- Two cups of plain beans
- One cup of chopped bacon
- Two cups of pasta
- Two tablespoons of chopped fresh herbs
- Chopped dill for servings

INSTRUCTIONS

1. Take a large saucepan.
2. Add the oil and onions into the pan.
3. Cook the onions until they turn golden brown.
4. Add the crushed garlic into the pan.
5. Add the beans, mixed greens and bacon into the mixture.
6. Add the vegetable stock, pasta and dried white wine.
7. Mix all the ingredients well and add the fresh herbs into the pan.
8. Cover the pan with a lid for five minutes.
9. Let the soup cook properly.
10. Season the soup with salt and black pepper.
11. Dish out the soup into soup bowls.
12. Add the chopped fresh dill on top.
13. The dish is ready to be served.

COOK TIME: 20 *mins*
SERVING: 4

CORSICAN LASAGNE

INGREDIENTS

- One cup of chopped onion
- One tablespoon of fresh dill
- Four teaspoons of olive oil
- One teaspoon of dried oregano
- Two cloves of chopped garlic
- Two cups of tomato paste
- Half cup of chopped mint leaves
- One cup of crumbled brocciu or ricotta cheese
- One pack of boiled lasagna sheets
- One cup of ground beef
- One teaspoon of salt
- One teaspoon of black pepper

COOK TIME: *30 mins*
SERVING: *4*

INSTRUCTIONS

1. Preheat the oven at 160 degrees.
2. Take a large pan.
3. Add the olive oil and onion.
4. Cook the onions until they turn soft.
5. Add the garlic into the pan.
6. Cook for about two to three minutes.
7. Add the beef and spices.
8. Mix well and then add the tomato paste.
9. Cook the ingredients well for ten minutes.
10. Take a baking dish and place some of the beef paste on it.
11. Add the lasagna sheets and brocciu cheese on top.
12. Make similar layers until all the ingredients finish.
13. Add the chopped mint leaves on top.
14. Bake the dish for about twenty minutes.
15. The dish is ready to be served.

ROUGETA A LA BONIFACIENNE

INGREDIENTS

- One pound red mullet pieces
- One teaspoon of kosher salt
- Two tablespoons of butter
- One teaspoon of black pepper
- Chopped parsley for serving
- One teaspoon of garlic powder
- Two celery stalks
- One cup of onions
- Two bay leaves
- One cup of red wine

COOK TIME: 35 mins
SERVING: 4

INSTRUCTIONS

1. Take a large pan.
2. Add the onions and butter into the pan.
3. Cook the onions well until they turn soft.
4. Add the red mullet, kosher salt, black pepper, celery stalks and garlic powder into the pan.
5. Cook the mullet for ten to fifteen minutes.
6. Add the bay leaves and red wine into the mixture.
7. Cook for ten more minutes.
8. Dish out the mullet.
9. Add the chopped parsley on top.
10. Your dish is ready to be served.

CIVET DE SANGLIER

INGREDIENTS

- Four cups of vegetable stock
- Two tablespoons of crushed garlic
- Salt to taste
- Black pepper to taste
- Two tablespoons of olive oil
- One cup of onion
- One cup of diced carrots
- One cup of chopped ham
- One bouillon cube
- Two tablespoons of chopped fresh herbs

COOK TIME: *20 mins*
SERVING: *4*

INSTRUCTIONS

1. Take a large saucepan.
2. Add the oil and onions into the pan.
3. Cook the onions until they turn golden brown.
4. Add the crushed garlic into the pan.
5. Add the carrots and ham into the mixture.
6. Add the vegetable stock and bouillon cube into the pan.
7. Mix all the ingredients well and add the fresh herbs into the pan.
8. Cover the pan with a lid for five minutes.
9. Let the mixture cook properly.
10. Season the dish with salt and black pepper.
11. Dish out the soup.
12. The dish is ready to be served.

GATEAU A LA FARINE DE CHATAIGNE

INGREDIENTS

- Half cup of butter
- One teaspoon of vanilla extract
- Two cups of chestnut flour
- Half cup of white sugar
- Two eggs
- A pinch of salt

COOK TIME: *30 mins*
SERVING: *12*

INSTRUCTIONS

1. Take a large bowl.
2. Add the butter, eggs and white sugar into the bowl.
3. Mix all the ingredients well to form a homogenous mixture.
4. Add the chestnut flour, salt, and vanilla extract slowly into the egg mixture.
5. Fold the mixture well.
6. Preheat the oven at 180 degrees.
7. Take a greased baking tray.
8. Add the cake mixture into the tray.
9. Place the baking tray into the oven.
10. Bake the cake for thirty minutes.
11. Dish out the cake when done.
12. Your dish is ready to be served.

Conclusion

The French are not lazy when it comes to food making. Meals are seen as a time to celebrate and socialize with friends or family. Snacking is not a big part of the French diet. An aperitif (alcoholic drink) or an afternoon tea may be the only form of snacking. According to studies, only about 15% of the French population snacks throughout the day. Despite the fact that their culture revolves around food, France has the highest life expectancy and the lowest obesity rate among Western countries.

This cookbook incorporates original recipes belonging to Paris, Île-de-France, Champagne, Lorraine, Alsace, Normandy, Brittany, Loire Valley, Central France, Burgundy, Franche-Comté, Bordeaux, Périgord, Gascony, Basque country, Provence-Alpes-Côte d'Azur, and Corsica categories. So, start cooking today with this delicious French cookbook!